TROUBLING ENTENDRES

—————————
—————————

TITUS CORLEONE

Contents

DEDICATION

I dedicate this book to the late, great Lee Rodgers.
In my opinion, Lee was the finest radio talk show
host in the country. I was hooked on his show from
the first time I tuned in, and that is where I learned
to be a conservative. Later on, Lee and I became pen
pals and he painstakingly tutored me on my writing
as I came up through the ranks in the blogging
world. He was a fine man and a great conservative,
and he is sorely missed by many, many admirers.
Thanks Lee

Preface

If you feel that something is seriously wrong with the direction America is going, then I am your poet. If you came up through elementary, middle, and high school knowing in your heart that many of the things your teachers were saying was flawed, then this book is for you. If you do not understand why most the media either ignores the important news, or manages it away, then know that I am their mocking jay, and I encourage you to become the new 4th Estate.

If you feel intense dismay and frustration at the Republican party leadership for refining surrender and betrayal to a high art form... then hear my rallying cry! Finally, if deep inside your gut you believe that for the past 35 years, one president after another has edged this country closer and closer to irreversible destruction...then Troubling Entendres contains your marching songs.

Though you will find conservative ideology reverberating throughout the poems like transverse waves upon a reflecting pool, this is not just a book of political poetry. You will find comedy, tragedy, love, hope, and bitter disdain as well. I have assembled a ménage of observations into the human condition along with a soliloquy or two for your reading pleasure. Be forewarned that many of my poems are meant to read like a marching cadence because I truly believe that Christian Conservatives are at war with a powerful enemy for the soul of America. That said; you will indeed find the ride an emotional roller coaster.

Troubling Entendres is my response to a maddened world… It is a scrolling marquee and I - the furious commentator.

The defining hallmark of poetry is verse that provokes the reader to emotion and imagery. Herein, the task is accomplished. As for repetition of similar sounds… I call upon my heroes - Frost, Poe, and Dickenson…

"promises to keep, and miles to go before I sleep"

"'Tis some visitor," I muttered, "tapping at my chamber door— only this and nothing more."

"and sore must be the storm - that could abash the little Bird that kept so many warm"

Finally, I'd like to touch upon my personal nature to sting at the left. I do harbor a frothy blood libel for Marxists because I am their natural enemy - a Christian Conservative and Patriot! If you are of the same ilk, then you're in good company. Damn the Godless Marxist!! There be no common ground with those foul running dogs, and Entendres will make them howl and salivate like Pavlov's dogs before driving them back into their own foul vomit...

Now, my good people this is key: I have an entirely different philosophy regarding those I term, "*Classic Liberals.*" I see many Liberals as tainted by the angry Left. However, there are millions more who have withstood the twisted temptations of Marx, Soros and Progressivism. This is because Classic Liberals are all about open mindedness, tolerance, and freedom. Conversely, the Left is defined by close mindedness, intolerance, and control. I strongly believe that before they began their war for the hearts and minds of America, Liberals and Conservatives were soul mates; a natural pairing; a true symbiosis... In fact, this I know: together, we built this mighty nation and it can't survive without both flavors. Therefore, Classic Liberals will find themselves very welcome and at home here......

So please, come and join me on the narrow path that God hath adorned so generously...

TC

A Pearl of Wisdom

A wise man's heart is at his right hand — His understanding or wisdom is always present with him, and ready to direct him in all his actions. He manages all his affairs prudently and piously. He mentions the right hand because that is the common instrument of action. But a fool's heart is at his left. His understanding and knowledge serve him only for idle speculation and vain ostentation, but is not useful or effectual to govern his affections and actions. Yea also, when he walketh by the way — not only in great undertakings, but in his daily conversation; his wisdom faileth him. His heart is wanting; he acts preposterously and foolishly, as if he were without a heart.

Ecclesiastes 10:2-3

- 1 -

The Chatterzees

I wrote The Chatterzees after being invited to an Ivy League fund raising event for a campaign to limit tuition increases.

My first impression was there probably wasn't a frat brother or sister in the house who hailed from stock unable to meet every expense of an Ivy League education... My second observation was, not a one of them had the vaguest clue why tuitions were so high. When I asked a young girl what she thought about the salaries, golden benefits, and platinum pension system of her professors, she vacantly replied, "What's that got to do with it?..." That was when I withdrew to a dark corner and began jotting down the first verses of The Chatterzees while observing in horror the generation that would soon run America...

***

O cheeky chatty simian pack;
Ivy cast tried and true
Clattery bliss and chirpy spats
Behold the den of pratteroos

I'm so spry – you're amazing!
We're the cleaver cheeky chatty class
Whipsawed tongues – minds a blazing
Hear the sermon lowly trash

Hawkish Sniping cliquish sects;
Acid drips off tip tongue cracks
We're the cleaver cheeky chatty class
We can't abide your smarmy smacks

Dare you traipse your clunky shtick
To the lively Ivy chatty clique?
We grasp the flush – you fold and blush
Quiet waif - you're not so slick…

Get thee hence, be quiet, sit
Absorb thee now our sprightly wisdom
Churchill Downs and Hampton wit
Knightsbridge too – and polo Lisbon

Little beast with tongue-tied speech -
See no, hear no, speak no fable
Presume thee we're the ones to teach?
Depart from we whilst thine still able!

A wavy armed warning fool
To never reach our Ivy mind -
For we're the cleaver, cheeky, pratteroos
With fox fur fleece and Golden hind

Thy speak of God and moral stands;
A nation under Son of Man?
The profit's tale pollutes the lands
Your morals back into the can!

Foolish waif - cease your cries
We grow weary of thy spry
Dare you stir our slaking lives?
Invoke our wrathful angered eye

Burn down Rome – no concern!
Devils crouching creeping glare;
Enemy armies mass and churn…
Our sight be veiled by mindless fare

For we're the cheeky chatty pinched face sour;
Wizened wizards with arched eyed glower
Entreat thee now – behold our power
Be quiet, behave, oh little flower!

Let it fall, let it fall …
The house comes down upon us all
If you be savior, sign post, warrior tall,
We hear thee not – your warning call

Dare thee dane to save our class?
You're not part and don't belong.
Thy have no stock in our charming cast
Away your mindless warning wax

From the devils den to soiree mass …
Into the night I strolled with heart of glass
They couldn't hear the lower class
As destruction tolled and danger massed
The sun set on the clever, cheeky, chatty class

***

- 2 -

Angel Eyes

Angel Eyes is a true story from a time when I didn't believe I'd ever find love.

Truly despondent, I called my father and he consoled me. Dad is gone now, but when he was alive he was always able to boil down my gravest problems into a solution encompassed in one sentence or less.

Pop was a hard bitten Sicilian loaded with salt-of-the-earth wisdom and values. You would have trouble these days finding a match for his morality too. In the 1950's he rose up through the ranks of the advertising world to become one of the true madmen. In fact, he was the last of them, and the world has been a lesser place with his departure.

Regarding true love, he worked his magic again - showing me the way forward with a few simple well placed words.

The problem of loneliness during my twenties was compounded by my absolute certainty I would spend the rest of my life in   a studio apartment and die alone. It was profoundly unnerving and depressing, and one time on the phone to dad I broke down, and he calmly uttered the magic words with absolute certainty, "*Son, your Angel Eyes will come soon...*" So I kept my heart true, prayed a lot, and in about a year she came when I least expected it.

This is my ode to the two I love most in this lonely cruel world: my wife, and my wonderful father. Thanks Dad...

***

> I laid my head upon father's shoulder
> Despair of life – I'm growing older
> Will my time come; the battle won?
> Or bleed my spirit in dreary dun...
>
> He dried my tears and soothed my hair
> Assured with words so simply done
> "You'll do great things my favored fair.
> Your deepest desires will soon be won..."
>
> I'll always remember his confident smile;
> Gentle eyes and mirthful guile.
> In time my soul would face the trial -
> But God was there all the while
>
> She came upon an evening psalm
> Beauty so pure – my heart did long!
> I did my best to wax manly strong
> Received my rose with binding thong
>
> My heart was tied by her angel eyes;
> My fate was sealed in sublime trance
> Father's words contained no lies

My time had come without askance
Oh my beautiful Angel Eyes!
Our path be one for all our lives
Father's words stand true and tried
My love at last and bright blue skies!

Hear my words, dry your tears
To a friend I wrote in true despair
Love will come I do declare!
Father's words were very clear

Angel Eyes made me – her love saved me
In God's good fortune she bathes me.
Our love, a timeless beautiful dream
Travails of life no power seen...
So know thee all in storm's careen
The world be cold, heartless, and mean
Yet father's wily mirthful grin
Evokes the God who hides all sin.

With faith in him who knows desire;
One day she'll come to love and sire
Angel and I paired - soul mates for life
Love under God – so sweet and right!

Knoweth I now the secret of father's smile
Like rising heights and soaring spires
The desires that heaven never denies
The faithful will find their Angle Eyes!

... Thanks Daddy...

***

- 3 -

McNessie of the Loch

We have a friend of Scottish decent who took a pilgrimage back to the old country.

Up in the highlands he met a stout young lass who decided to woo him, and indeed, she went after him with relentless vigor... He barely managed his escape back stateside and upon his return we met for dinner. After a little too much wine, he related the harrowing story of his encounter with the fearsome McNaught...

As the horrific tale rolled off his lips; his struggle with the randy lass took on hairs of such intensity that it drove us into hysterics. We began to drink, and drink hard, and between shots we concocted a rye limerick - foisting each stanza upon him in loud boasts... We laughed so hard our cheeks hurt and the staff and patrons thought we were mad! That was the genesis of McNessie of the Loch.

Amazing what a couple of martinis can do chased with some respectable Pinot. On that night we truly advance the art... Well, there you have it...

***

Who's the creature of the loch?

Slimy serpent or Nessie McNaught?
Fine example of Highland Stock
Corncob pipe and bristling legs
Sardonic grin and eyes like eggs
A heady lass who can't be tamed
Pop she walnuts in armpit mane
Haunts the glens – drives lads insane

Who's the creature of the loch?

She prowls by day and hunts by night
McSweens and Stewards take to flight!
Young Scoots virtue in peril tonight
McNessie's need – a ravenous might
Her fishy stink brings fearsome fright
Another Steward off the roll
Nessie's taken this week's toll

Who's the creature of the loch?

Over the glen come hither ye men
Highland charge check banshee whim
McSweens and Stewards battle the sin
Nessie slay all but just two men …
A Steward n' McSween the cornered hens
O monster spare us thy withering glare
She smacks the Steward and grabs his hair
McSween counters with shillelagh whack
Beer stein rocks her Glengarry cap
McNessie falls to darkest depths

Who's the creature of the loch?

Tell the children of Nessie's fall
Not Steward virtue after all…
'Twas mean ass McSween who met the call
Scourge of Eire to Nessie's gall
This is how the story ends
He fished her out and made amends
Repaired her noggin at McSween hall
Now Nessie and Sweeney have it all!!

Wee monsters soon for Loch Ness shoals…

***

- 4 -

Midie's Opine

Okay, it's a take-off from Seinfeld, 76th episode, "The Stall..." but I told Jerry I'd never recite it on a college campus...

***

Maddening dash to dingy stall
Waxing moan as great one falls
Groping grasp but TPs lapsed
What the hell to do?

Fretful plea to Lefty's stall
"A little help – one square is all
I've got a sitch' o can you spare...
Slip me under just one square"

Lefty twills and purses lips
supplies are low where she sits
"Perhaps to right make your plea
My need is greater can't you see?"

Tension mounts in Midi's stall
A knock upon Righty's wall
"Kindly grant me this one deed
I'm in itching drying chaffing need"

Righty snarls, "how do you dare?
Just one square I cannot spare
Were we not allotted equal shares?
Mine are mine I do declare!"

Midi whines and dawns a wince
"You selfish snots – get thee hence
To use ones hair makes better sense
A pox upon your shabby tents"

A silence falls on all three stalls
Midi's hand the final call
She exits fast and wipes the wall
For faucets broke no water falls

Midi leaves with burning tears
A chuckle utters from her peers
"Hey Sally, just imagine the whinny pout?
We did it again - let's clock out…"
Another ripper for the happy hour sisters

***

- 5 -

Native Grace

During one of the most desperate times in my life, I found myself in the horrifying position of being without a job (*thanks to the economic wizards in Washington...*)

The market was so tight that even with years of experience and training, I could not get work. I had to go back to school to get certificates and degrees so I could compete with thousands of other people looking for work. Many of the people who should have been helping us: friends, family, clergy... turned their backs on us.

We were desperate and in danger of losing our house. We had already lost our life savings and inheritances.

With bankruptcy looming, I was tipped off by a beautiful Christian woman about a medical clinic that served the Native American community. They were looking for someone to fill a part time position. They hired me and things began to change.

What I discovered was, they are the most gracious, beautiful people I've ever known, and my life was enriched working with them. I love them all. They saved us from eminent disaster – pulled us back just before we went over the edge into the abyss, and I'll never forget them for that.

The Native Americans handed us back our lives and Native Grace is my woefully deficient attempt to render heartfelt thanks to the wonderful Indian Nations.

***

One time in the past, my wit at its last,
and no one would offer us help…
No father nor mother; conservative or liberal;
not even a brother, pastor nor pagan,
would lend us a hand.

My best friend failed; abandoned the pact;
to face every storm back to back – the blood of my
heart was spilt
I prayed with my wife as horror encroached,
soon to lose all – perhaps even my life,
as drained out the final hour glass sand…

Though in the darkest hour, our situation so dour,
an angel named Connie came to say...
"There's five Indian Tribes who might take you in,
20 hours a week to prove you belong."
Hat in hand, I entered their land,
and sternly they charged,
"We'll try you out day to day..."

I took up the charge, worked well and worked hard,
and in time I discerned right from wrong…

So my people, I'd like you to see,
when the helping hand comes
you might never believe – who addresses your need
For God is everywhere and never forsakes,
he'll hold you up, and just might set you down
with a glorious Indian tribe

In our fearful hour they stood strong and in power;
extended their hand and from disaster we were freed
Take a lesson from your stormy lives,
for when your time comes –
behold what God provides,
and don't be surprised…

From our hearts, thank you Indian Nations

***

- 6 -

Empty Corner

Over the years I have suffered the loss of loved ones to the sands of time. This gave rise to an acute observation about the human condition… It is truly a dance, the celebration of life, the tragedy of loss, the permanence of death.

The stark truth is that if we're not careful, our circle of companions will shrink over time – and this is especially true for those who forgo the joy of procreation… However, my Christian faith reminds me of the promise of eternal life…

Even if we end up dying old and alone, the happy times are immortalized safe in our hearts and, providing we make the right choices, all will be relived again in heaven. We must hold dearly to this faith, and each time we despair over the loss of a loved one, we must remember that this brief splash of life is but a drop in the sea of eternity… Choose God and I promise you will soon be reunited with those you love. Empty Corner is my defiant retort to the Grim Reaper…

***

Yard parties, dinner parties, Christmas Eve, and
New Year's cheer
Such merriment from young, old, dull, and fair
Happy throngs revel as my heart dishevels...
Fun filled havoc and mess
Inconvenient stress – curse the RSVP – self-
punishment I see!

Duty calls, soldier on, serve more wine,
trampled lawn...
So many here I do declare - Every corner under the
dormer is filled I fear

Teresa, Marco, Hank, and Uncle Frank
Kathy's laugh and Ron seems tanked. Music roars to
laughing hoards
Kids be smeared in frosting cake - Rosie screams of
mess they make
Bad jokes, gaffs and roaring laughs
And yes, forever, we thought all would last

Then one Christmas grief and dread
An empty corner – we're short one head
So long taken for granted – Uncle Joe is dead...
Under the dormer our first empty corner

Mask the pain and soldier on, but something's
missing, someone's gone
I wish I'd adored his presence more – value forsaken
– heart strings torn

Easter fells winter and flowers bloom
A gathering called to banish gloom
But wait I say – the count be low
Now we're missing Auntie Roe
Winters wrath hath taken toll
And under the dormer one more empty corner

Mask the pain and soldier on, yet another's
missing, one more gone
I wish I'd adored her presence more - value forsaken
– heart strings torn

A shrinking circle at horrific cost
Another library to decay and moth
Chin up - Easter Egg Hunt - but child decries
"Where's Auntie Roe to help find my prize?"
Apologies made and tendered lies
She shows she knows in streaming tears
A child's intuition makes all so clear
That under our dormer… there is… one more
empty corner

Mask the pain and soldier on, but more go missing,
now many gone
I wish I'd adored their presence more – value forsaken
– heart strings torn

Now we see the dreadful thing
Barbeque call but one more falls
The loss is felt - joy is squelched

Our aging clan reels from death's tightening belt
Marco's loss is felt
And under the dormer now so many empty corners
I think with sadness of ages past
Granted taken as lives forsaken
Loved ones value – silence sallow
"Will I be last?" I think aghast!
I should have loved harder under the dormer
For now the Reaper hath silenced every corner...

Age and frailty - end my torture!
I pray for strength but will it come?
"Be silent!" beckons the Holy One...
Welcoming spirits in every corner?
Death and sorrow retreat from light
I raise my eyes to hopeful sights
The promise kept in heavenly heights
Reveling noise – a party rages
Heavenly hosts from all the ages
Loved one's free from bodily cages
Mother, Father, my beautiful Wife
Friends of old – the spirits entice
Vanquished pain and banished strife!

Behold the glow of Heavens dormer
Eternal Joy in every corner

***

- 7 -

American Dreamer

I wrote American Dreamer while helping my dearest friend to die.

Each day as he grew more ill, I spoke with him about God, Jesus, salvation – and the promise of eternal life. Sadly, I do not think he received the message. I believe he took a pass on committing himself to God. To me, that was the most horrifying and painful part of his passing.

We all live sinful lives, but being perfect is not a requirement for entrance into heaven. In a moment of grace, if we merely bend a knee before Jesus Christ, confess, and pray for salvation – He will faithfully welcome us in. However, this poem portrays the horrific alternative…

I loved my friend, and I know he was a good person, but that is not all it takes. Anyone who truly has not heard of the Lord can be saved by grace, but those who did hear and turned away – well… I'll just say they're in for a horrible surprise. For I know. I've been there…

I was on the edge of the abyss a couple of times myself and God, doctors, or perhaps my own stubborn will pulled me back before it was too late. In those brief moments at the abyss, I saw there were only two options – and I had chosen the wrong one... I know now, there is a heaven and hell, and definitely no second chance once we've shed our mortal bodies.

I urge you, if you haven't already - make the choice now... Choose the Lord and his Son, because what is coming is permanent and you don't want to bet against eternity...

***

I live each day as if in a dream - consumed by the
trifles of my little sphere.
Not once to ponder things unseen - taking my
pleasures with nether a care...

Now who's the man standing at my door? I feel such
shame and bone chilling dread.
What does he mean, "I have time no more?" Surely I
can't be dead!

I do recall this man - his story a bore. Yet so piercing
a stare; right into my soul.
They taught he was myth, nothing more. Now
plainly I see, he truly is Lord...

As a tear rolled down his cheek he pronounced,
"I never knew you I do declare.
A thousand signs but you never cared.
From crib to school and through your career,
I was always there. Yet you chose the world and now
you've had your share."

Enormous peril I see I'm in.
A chasm below takes root within.
Summon all my skills to evade the sling,
I'll negotiate with this man till now unseen.
Lord, I admit I'm no stranger to sin, but I be not the
worst of tawdry men.
I beg thee now, save me from the encroaching
dark thing!

And in an instant I knew my case was lost,
and I too late.
In a blink of an eye he recited my entire life …
"You never mocked me – yet your indifference; was
the final expression of hate.
The gulf between us pierced my heart as with a
knife."

I felt his countenance stripping all the good left;
laying my soul bare.
Each and every lost opportunity suddenly flashed
through my head.
Oh please Lord, allow me now to show I care!
Sentence pronounced – eternally dark, blackness
engulfs, my soul be dead…

"You've made your bed dreamer, now off you go.
I summon my children in your stead…"

**Think a little every day about eternity, perilous
indifference, and God.**

***

29

- 8 -

Things In A Drawer

The genesis of this poem is very personal... We'll just leave it at this: there are many ways to become a parent, and many ways to lose a child. As for the latter, it leaves a terrible scar upon the soul. The worst thing is to be left behind, and no parent should ever suffer the loss of their baby. Yet many do, and it lays waste to lives... Worse yet, is the dark day when evil raises to torture those left behind in the form of painful reminders – perhaps a forgotten item in a kitchen drawer... An accusing little toy that caused the loss of a child.

There is no telling what damage a little token from the past can cause. They have the power to bring back memories, some happy, others sad, a few dangerous... Things in a Drawer is about a man's brief warm time before all his hopes and dreams are dashed upon the rocks. It is about a monstrous little object that tears open a scar from the past bringing a nightmare back to life - to claim one more victim.

Endure till the end of this poem, because indeed, there is hope even in the midst of the darkest day...

***

Another frigid stark winter's day
My pains pronounced;

Ambled the house
How to while the hours away?
Seeking matches to light my smoke
Rifled drawers in hutch and den
Surveyed the pantry, emptied bins
Then spied I a seldom visited kitchen drawer

Feeling ill, I quietly drew the pull
With deep foreboding in my soul
I sensed a painful journey to days of old
And then, my blood ran cold

My eyes beheld gaggles of forgotten doilies,
Candles, and cloths of cotton
Taken aback on yesteryear's wings
I gazed upon the dreaded thing

A child's toy
Days filled with joy
I think he was seven
Now gone to heaven

As gazing through frosted glass
I remember the bright warm storefront
Beheld from the freezing cold
My blood ran to ice – as the memory told

Great joy I had in those days of old
Fatherhood fulfilled – such a happy time
But the toy in the drawer – darkness told
Come hither my baby; the Reaper's rhyme

Cursed little car sealed his fate

He tossed the thing over the gate
And into the street he met his fate
My boy to the angels and I to living hell

The moral of my darkest day
Covet thy love and precious moments
Never pass on a chance for joy
For the Reaper may come in the form of a toy

As I wiped my tears, a burning arose
Pain like lighting and great alarm
Then blinding light and scents of rose
"Daddy, you're home and safe from harm!"

My boy had come to take me home
No more empty days and crying nights
Darkest lonely desperate plight
Through heaven's gate we strolled that night
And all I lost was in my sight

Enjoy your times before they're gone
Love all ye can with fierce might
And know thine heart in the darkest hour
God hath made you a creature of the light
The days of your grief he hath numbered
And saved thee eternity in bejeweled slumber

Hold On

***

- 9 -

Trayvon Gone

An absolute fury boiled up in me over the sheer stupidity of the Trayvon/Zimmerman tragedy. Trayvon, like any other kid, had nothing but promise yet no one was there to help him channel it into something positive. Zimmerman was simply an idiot who appointed himself Sheriff, and quickly found himself in way over his head.

So you have a kid with a temper and a mean right hook. He was probably on his way to being a hood anyway... then the moron playing cop... hog-legging it around the neighborhood with a gun.

The result: Trayvon lost is life and Zimmerman's was ruined. Eternal shame on the later, and I lament the, "*might-have-been*" with Travon...

Trayvon Gone is my heartfelt notion of what might have been. Trayvon could have made it into professional football and Zimmerman actually had aspirations to become a venture capitalist and develop large properties. Under different circumstances, how might it have gone? Hmmm, who knows?....

***

Trayvon's gone - where did he go?
Life quest lost in anger's flow
Where is Trayvon – do you know?
Zimmered blast to Satan's stow

Sin's reign is lawlessness
People cower in humble nests
Utopian rule a Marxist mess
Give rise to Zimmer's deadly best

I will ascend to lofty quests
Save my king's lowly guests
Garda – Ranger – Batman one
Destroy intruders with my gun!
Where is Trayvon – prodigal son?

Left winged knight gives troubled sigh
Trayvon spied with evil eyes
Griffin or Phoenix, one to die
Battles on with sissy cries;
Griffin walks and Phoenix lies

Where is Trayvon – do you know?
Angry lusty life out flows
Zimmered Knight struck the blow
Trayvon's gone and Zimmer's crowed
A fleeting flash in Satan's show

Trayvon - Zimmer what's the cost?
Wasted life - potential lost!
Utopian charges – both are crossed

Sin still reigns in evil's frost;
People cower and deny the cross

When capitalism thrives – crime is low
Potential soars when money flows
God given rights would save the knights
Zimmer a winner at broker's dinners
Trayvon takes the running pass...
Zimmer ventures stadiums rise
Who knows - Trayvon wins a Super bowl prize!

The ring of glory in hero's hand
Shinning stadium with capital stands
A hero's glory in monumental edifices
Another outcome, o' you incredulous!
With potential, both might have won
Remanded now to Satan's sons
Zimmer brought down low - and...

Where is Trayvon – do you know?

***

- 10 -

My Fleur-De-Lys

Cards on the table... I'm a Christian, and a conservative, and a patriot. Declarations made, I still believe that any free nation requires a mix of conservatives and "classic-liberals" to truly prosper and maintain freedom. We need both wings to make the nation soar. However, since the early 1900's there has been destabilizing poison injected into the ether of western civilization. I call it Leftism, but it is really the cancer of free peoples the world over, and has afflicted mankind since the dawn of civilization...

True liberals are about freedom and unity. conservatives are about structure and the rule of law. Together, we built the most mighty, prosperous and free nation on the face of the earth. Sadly, by the mid-1960's liberals were seduced in ever increasing numbers by the Leftist message of division, intolerance, and control. Today they are running the nation into the ground. My mother was a classic liberal. My father a Christian conservative and I have parts of both.

We need this balance for America to survive, but we don't need Leftism. I personally believe the Left is trying to destroy America and I unabashedly state

that we need to show them the door. So, in defense
of the realm…

***

What can I tell thee of my Fleur-de-lys…? Come
hither ye children and listen to me.
It began with the oppressed who hoped to be free;
they gathered their shillings and set to the sea.
A promise of liberty to prodigal sons - to distant
shores they sailed this core.
With great courage they struggled to settle and store
- a hundred battles were fought and won.
Yet Plymouth rock proved not promise; but disease,
scourge, mosquitoes and mud.
Fields were furrowed, and sown with blood –
though in time, the flower's children basked in the
sun.

My Fleur-de-lys be a perfect flower – yet a thing that
is sensed and rarely seen.
Holy spirit shine on her from above; her
countenance a gift to hearts of good will.
She's the spirit of hope, freedom, thrift and love;
the lady's torch true and clean.
Liberty and abundance the flower provides, might
and power our foundation astride.
A bounty that wolves seek to divide, and enemies
glowered – cowards unseen…Now perk ye ears for
this be key, the monsters discovered new ways to
bind.

Other ways they scheme today, abide they not her
good works in motion.
It's the back door, my children, the darkness seeks.
Infect young minds with rancid potion…

The flower's children endangered with deadly
passions and deceitful notion;
into the patina inject they their poison; weaken
young men with mind numbing dope.
Sow they selfish need, apathy and greed – entitled
division the standard they bear.
From the flower flow tears as her thrifty children
abandon all hope

And soon cometh the day with intent to confound;
enemies surround her.
As they tear, scratch, and cloy - her underpinnings
tremor.
Yet know ye, in the darkest hour – all is not lost!
Gather I say you, mighty steeds bray, sabers a
rattling… roil forth with great might.
Unhand her you monsters! Strike at the heart – slay
the dividers with truth bearing darts.
On that golden day – the flower of life will be
saved…

The enemy be lawyers, thieves and agency monsters;
plying usurious fees …
While rage wells in good men's hearts, abiding not in
the evil way.

Back away! Back Away! Unhand her I say - strike
thee at the monster's heart.
Sally forth men of good will; destroy them all on the
golden day, the flower we must save!
For they be children of the raven, unnaturally
craven; given charge of the jewels and crown.
Banish them all I say! Into the fray! Drive them
back to the dark lord's cave…

Push them below on the dark winding road that only
leads down to evil's abode.
For we are the nation of the flower shinning forth
God's great power.
Restore He when pleased with us – love His son
Jesus – who heals the land.
And for a thousand more years America will stand.
This be the story of my beautiful Fleur-de-lys…

So my children now you see, you be the hope of a
nation eternally.
Muster you good and mighty; allow them no more to
divide us! The matter is decided…
And when the battle is won, hear the cry from
above, the flower begs - return to me!
Black, white, brown and yellow: derive us – her army
stands united – for we are one under God's blazing
sun…

Remember the great battle when deceived evil
chattel be destroyed or freed!

The forces of good, on the ramparts they stood;
between evil and the flower.
Never forget my brave little knights, excise the evil
before it takes root.
Save my Fleur-de-lys from evil cowards! Bind their
works with fearsome power.
Away from our shores, back away! Cleanse the
nation of the black hearted soot.

And now, I lay down my armor and sword…
knowing the enemy yields.
For if ever again she bleeds or is weak, her
wonderful children will mend her;
A new generation protects the great seal, and bears
me to rest up their shields.
Tears be dried, moth and dust cleansed – America
stands another thousand years.
Into her heart my spirit flows, the nation stands tall
and Fleur-de-lys glows…
As I breathe my last; eyes gleaming with joy; to you
children I say – no crocodile tears

Always Protect the Fleur-de-lys

***

- 11 -

The Ameratoosee

The Ameratoosee takes its place somewhere between "Itsy Bitsy Spider" and "The Hokey Pokey." It may even be for your kids to deprogram their friends. It is a comic sing-along mocking the politically correct, with suggestions on how the races might reject the dividers and come back together. On a serious note, I took inspiration from my friend's son, who was a very Caucasian looking Sicilian kid who was attacked by a gang of Sicilians because they thought he was a northern Italian. I think it is high-time that we get a handle on our own racial mess in America before all is lost...

***

I looked up in a tree and what did I see?
A huge piñata swinging down at me!
I grabbed my shalaylee and gave it one square hit
Now we munching candy with the Mexican chicks

Oh America, can't you see?
Racial divides the land of the free
We all bleed red – Liberty's sons
E Pluribus Unum - from many into one!

Well I looked up in a tree and what did I see?
A scared black guy whispering, "help me please!"

I gave the cops a shout – he didn't rob the house
Now every Friday we pick'n wings at da house

Oh America, can't you see?
All we have is equality
Welcome men of color into your hood
It'll save the country and make you feel good!

I checked my boy's school to see if all was cool
Spied a Marxist teacher acting like a fool
Stomping the flag and quoting lefty rags
I called her out – the screeching old hag

Oh America, can't you see?
Hate my country same as hating me
Teaching discontent – Marxist doctrine's bent
In the land of plenty blessed with God's good sense!

Spring come along and I go to mow my lawn
A little Asian kid asks if he can have the job
I get us lemonade and show him how to blade
Now I got another friend and the chore is made

Oh America, can't you see?
Young people brimming with energy
Let em do the grounds and we better all around
One step closer to a big Boy's Town

I look down my street and what do I see
Narco gangs moving in on me
They give my kids drugs cause they're just a bunch
of thugs

We stand against evil and give the good hugs

Oh America, can't you see?
Saving the children - saves you and me
Fight the dark hoards - push em overboard
Beat the heathen back or our future to the sword

I watch the T.V. and what did I see
My g-stringed daughter up on MTV
My little angel's gone – now a sleazy slouch
Hollywood wrecked her on the casting couch

Oh America, can't you see?
If we abandon God we lose everything
Tricked us with their porn – values were scorned
Don't give a rat's ass? Well, now you've been warned...

Now everywhere I look evil abounds
The wealthy and famous have set the traps
I'm tired of their sewage and turning off the tap
Gonna boot their butts and shut their little yaps

Oh America, you should be disturbed
Time to kick the Left straight to the curb
No more silence or look the other way
Take the country back – DO IT TODAY!

***

**If the world is the Titanic, then America has
become the lifeboat. The problem is the lifeboat
is now full, and it is we now who are in danger**

of sinking. Therefore, we need to repel boarders, but that does not mean we can't go out into the world and help people to keep their own nations afloat...

Long live America

***

- 12 -

The God Of Self

I press in again on the dangers of our not coming together as one people.

America has jealous rabid enemies on all sides. They were never able to beat us on the battlefield or economically, but from within? That's a different story. If we allow them to corrupt all our institutions and morality, we will all lose…

***

Oh mighty nation, how could they have known
Seeds of destruction so cleverly sown
Their bountiful garden baptized by lightning and
thunder
To suffer blight and be torn asunder

They cast the die of hope – Godly assuredness
Freedom's redoubt; crucible e pluribus
Of all the world's sullied travails
She would save us – her people prevailed

Oh innocent folk of blessed nation
They died for liberty – to eradicate station
E pluribus unum from fractured mosaic
indelible success to sadly prosaic

They forgot the wolves circling freedom's light
The cowardly pack from darkest night
Trappings of luxury dimmed their sight
A thousand cuts - their eyes shut tight

Hearts will fail on the darkest day
They did not see the enemy's ways
E Pluribus Unum to E Pluri Divide
Blows cast down - as the great ones hide

The land born of courage and hope;
Destroyed by greed and bound with evil rope
Another thousand years of darkness and plight
When America descends back into the night

Oh you poor people hear my plea
Awake, awaken from your slumber!
The danger encircles can't you see?
Reject the dividers with God's great thunder

Throw off your luxurious distractions
The alternative's too horrible to imagine
Return to God – reject the factions
To save our home requires your action!

Sharia law and corporate statists
Purveyors of porn – know they hate us
They'll burn down our entire house
Our courage reduced to a shivering mouse

Will we find that amazing courage?
A path away from destructive scourge
Reject porn, drugs, and divisive ruin
A return to unity – e pluribus unum!

Another thousand years the flame will burn
From America's path the enemies turn
They fear and covet our brightest light
Love of God and moral might

From circling wolves to warming pelts
From Euros, Africans, Hispanics we melt
Fractured mosaic to bronzed sword and shield
God over America - never to yield…

The only color that matters is red.
Awaken!

***

- 13 -

Helpless Rocks

I try to watch all the major news networks: NBC, CNN, ABC, and FOX. I want to hear it from every side.

There is a guy on FOX you may know named Waters. He conducts "man on the street" interviews. Waters polls people to check their awareness on various political and social issues.

I believe in compassion, but Waters does a brilliant job of making something glaringly clear: the average American's lack of knowledge regarding civics, politics, and current events is horrifying! I remember a time when people weren't led like sheep. Up to the 1960's most Americans were well informed on these subjects and the fact that they no longer are, I believe, is very much by design. Dumbing down the populace is part and parcel of the Leftist play book, and they have succeeded in blinding many Americans. It is up to us to "reeducate" the people.

The second part to this is, today we are now trillions of dollars in debt from excessive entitlements which cannot be sustained. In a few short years we will be at what I call, "the zero point" where our payments on the debt and the interest charged, will be greater than the nation's entire GDP. Getting out of debt will then be impossible for America and we will be at the mercy of our creditors. American is teetering at the edge of the abyss and our children and grand-children are in terrible jeopardy.

To the oblivious, I give you this …

***

I'm a helpless rock - can't count to three
Politics just ain't for me
A dumb blind brick with iPhone free…
But I got self-esteem - oh golly gee!

School wunt no help – a hop-scotch whelp
Math Appreciation - my brains be spilt
But Mary Jane paved my way
to the Strato Lounge and Frito Lays

Ohhhhhh, I'm a helpless rock - can't count to three
Politics just ain't for me
A dumb blind brick with iPhone free…
But I got self-esteem - oh golly gee!

But when I'm bored I know what ta do
Ma sex ed tips with motley fools
Afta high school college was cool
Signed up for Zen study tools

Learned protest chants and Marxist rants
An da girls done boot me out of Feminist Camp

Why... I'm a helpless rock - can't count to three
Politics just ain't for me
A dumb blind brick with iPhone free...
But I got self-esteem - oh golly gee!

Ah can't get work and life just stinks
I'm a welfare fraud and food stamp fink
They offer free stuff - I'm at the trough
I look in the mirror - gag and cough
It's only now that I see
The entire nation's just like me!

Because... I'm a helpless rock - can't count to three
Politics just ain't for me
A dumb blind brick with iPhone free...
But I got self-esteem - oh golly gee!

No mo money left frum gubament dole
EBT card - now on hold
Time to join the panicked mass
Cause sure as hell my ass is grassed

Annnnd - I'm a helpless rock - can't count to three
Politics just ain't for me
A dumb blind brick with iPhone free...
But I got self-esteem - oh golly gee!

Let the Chinese in to take care of me

Slaves for cash but Doritos r' free
Freedom's gone but who cares Jack?
I'm a helpless rock but my welfare's back
Set me right down in a labor camp
Work rice paddies in stripy pants
Singing Marxist songs as the oxen cants

Ohhhhh I'm a helpless rock - can't count to three
Politics just ain't for me
A dumb blind brick with iPhone free…
But I got self-esteem - oh golly gee!

Chinese know we got brains of toad
They just struck gold on the Marxist road
Built our solar panels and made our tanks
Thought we were pals but the whole thing stank
Defaulted on the debt and they took our banks
To the useful idiots - we got no thanks!

Miss my Frito Lays and Top Raman stanks!

***

- 14 -

The College Of Political Knowledge

I wrote this after my first year of college...

The bias of most my professors was overwhelming, infuriating, and scary. I have no ax to grind with much of academia, but for me, the Rubicon was crossed when I personally witnessed Left Wing professors steeped in anti-American ideology, abuse their power in order to corrupt innocent young minds.

In American today, I believe these same leftists and progressives are in Hollywood, television, cable T.V., the music industry, the internet, as well as our schools. Their mission is to pollute and destroy the wholesome American values handed down to us from our forbearers. This is a weakening and diluting process right out of Saul Alinsky's "Rules for Radicals." They are at war with religion, tradition, thrift, and self-sufficiency. They are using Satan's vile tools to ruin America: sex, hedonism, and the rejection of Christian values and/or any notion of God. They are trying to condition our children's thoughts and manage out any useful news.

Most people I've spoken with whose eyes are not open say they feel helpless against the power of academia and the broadband sewer pipe dripping into their living rooms. I assure them they are not alone, and that 200 million Americans face the same plight. I tell them what I'm telling you right now: this battle will be won one soul at a time. I believe we should demand that the entertainment providers be forced to offer Cable a la Carte. Only then will the people be empowered to punish offending networks by having the ability to simply drop offending channels.

Another idea would be to make it illegal for educators to expound their political or social philosophies in the classroom.

We must demand the return of unbiased education in all taxpayer funded institutions...

Obviously, another potent weapon is writing. We can beat the left at their own game by blogging, adding our thoughts to the comments section of articles, and through the mediums of art and poetry. They can fight us, but they can't fight words and ideas that instill courage, love of God, and patriotism from sea to shining sea.

So, without further ado, to the arrogant left wing asses of academia...

***

We are the college of political knowledge
Right the nation's wrongs!
Displaced compassion, calls to action
Division our siren's song…
Our mission molds young children's minds
Parental oblivion – not to worry – all is fine
A witches' caldron of evil swirls
We make your boys into little girls
And man up girls in crisp tight columns
Our bright red doctrine now unfurled

We're driving a wedge – your values to bed
Utopian credo slammed into their heads
Extol all desires - societal mires
In young minds we ignite brush fires

Attack the tenants – yesteryear's lore
Slaughter the lions by turning the pride
Bring down the leaders with Babylon's whores
Normal is horrible and deviance soars

Humiliation our weapon –white males belie
Destroyer of families – in the open we hide
Hand us your children to alter their minds
Over and over repeat the lies

We are the College of Political Knowledge
Planet is warming – with reindeer swarming
Don't ask! Believe the lies…

Benghazi from the video took four lives;
"What difference does it make?" - the Hildabeast
cries.

Hear the voice which hides our work
20 trillion on 40 million jerks
The working man to pay the bills
Then China comes to drill our wells
And when they take their lumber due
They'll strip the earth with mining crews

Remember the useful idiots who cheered them on
Enslaved their minds with siren songs
They paved our way with the magic runes
Death to the cops – their marching tune

We are the college of political knowledge
Enslave the men in Satan's crews
EU, Russia, China, to get their due
From days of old, the lofty goal – America dead
Then you'll know the Greens were Reds…
Soros, Khomeini and Putin - so shrewd

and American Christians lose their heads

***

- 15 -

Blazing Jon Boyner

I hope my conservative brethren understand this... The Republican party leaders are not conservatives. Even though the mainstream media would have us believe there are two distinct choices for the American people, I am here to say, unequivocally, there is not.

The leaders of the Republican party are the handmaidens of the corporate boardroom. They are the darlings of the U.S. Chamber of Commerce. They are anything but conservative or Christian in nature. They serve the interests, not of hardworking mainstream middle class families and businesses, but the Fortune 500 and multinational conglomerates. They will not take a stand against Obamacare because, truth-be-told, if we taxpayers take over paying benefits for the corporations ... would that not serve their bottom line better? They refuse to take stands on border security because that would get in the way of cheap labor. They refuse to adopt IRS reform because they are actually big-government-statist.

You can simply throw out any notions of sovereignty too. Notice how Boehner, McConnell, McCain and the rest rallied behind Obama on the

Trade Deal – even when Pelosi and the unions were against it. Why? Because they are not conservatives; not true Christians; not defenders of American sovereignty and exceptionalism. They merely pay lip-service to all that. They couldn't articulate conservative Christian values to anyone because they have no moral foundation and no ideological compass…

Therefore, it becomes necessary to express exasperation and fury at these compromised fools. Here you go…

***

Oh boy… oh boy … here I go… for the annals of history wax my prose
I dare not speak with classic skill, or mimic Cruz's angry shrill…
Another Jameson in the cup, hmmm… I'll probably muck the whole thing up
Whom shall I model? What to tell? Eureka, by golly, the ringing bell!

Yeah man! Here we go; I know I know… rolls off the tongue - Toastmaster's laud!
For the kids and old folk I'll champion cause… then pause… for applause… they'll teem!
Tug heartstrings, shed some tears, hmmm… more Jameson please…
Note to self… five more jars of tanning cream.

Here we go… here we go.
*"May the fruits of our labors be ladders our children can use
to blast off to the stars!"*

I'm so bright, fine and good. Would Reagan pale in
my stead?
Churchill, well… he'd kick me out of bed.
That said, I'll certainly ooze with charm and power!
Has the Jameson gone to my head?

*Sari, reserve me forty-five in the tanning booth at the Capital
Gym…*
Beat Marco and Rand to the sauna too… bounce a
check, it's no sin.
Dazzling bronze copper tan – they'll surly see I'm
the man…
What marvelous qualifications, *hmmm… I think I'll
switch to gin…*

Now for all the conservative trolls – if you think we
elites are getting old…
Silly quaint little men – our charter be the
Fortune 500.
Co-opt them into the chamber's fold. Forget that
damn old parchment, I say!
No matter how much we blunder – we'll tear the
middle class asunder.
Surely, I'm the prez they seek – Ben Carson be too
meek and mild.
Deliver the nation to the corporate Lords.

What helpless rocks the masses are.
Just mind the stock, unemployment rocks and let the
hoard run wild.

Not to worry, favors curried, the bottom line be my
family stone…
A thousand chairmen – I declare man, accountability
will hold!
American Corporation – Corporate America, our
bible be the "Recap of Block Control."
Jameson for me, America for Inc., I'll be the prez
when the nation's sold…

Time to kick the elites to the curb!

***

- 16 -

The Mocking Jay

I wrote the Mocking Jay after the 2008 election when I realized how incredibly biased the mainstream media had become. I asked myself, "How could this be?"

I reviewed all the debates and thousands of bytes of interview video and press coverage. The more I dug, the greater my feeling that something was terribly wrong. I felt like a boxer swinging out in all directions against a hundred opponents. That is how bad things have become. When I saw Romney and Ryan setup and take a deliberate fall, I knew I was not imagining things. Who was behind this?

The truth is that the Republican party leadership has been completely compromised and corrupted by the Democrats. DNC opposition research simply found their weaknesses and exploited them. First Gingrich, then Sanford, Trent Lott, Boehner, and McConnell – just to name a few. It may be too late to fix this but our hope should be in Christianity, the conservative movement, the Tea Parties, and intelligent classic liberals.

The GOP leadership has been corrupted by agents provocateurs of the DNC, and they clearly own the once great 4th estate (the news media.). However, we can still do the media's job, if they won't. I'm living proof of that. One way or another, we will win.

The spirit of America will endure. Trust the Mocking Jay on this one…

***

The fully sullied politician's screech
Believe us when we tell you, sell you, and change your mind…

Your reasoned logic we seek to breach
We broker not truth but lies to speak
Our dire hope your mind be weak…

On what you should know, the veil we drop
Lowered curtain – your mind be cropped…

Hear my words and watch the hand
O' little people pay us slack
See not the truth behind our backs
In deception we hold a clever knack…

With sleight of hand, a cloak we place
Seek to hide our master's face
Believe when we tell you, sell you – *oh, it's the other party*
Follow you now our master race…

Crossword puzzles and baby nuzzles, we parse thee
words in one ear
and fill the other with managed fear…
Distraction, obfuscation, and altered truths
In your mind the lies take root...

We count the course of your harried life
And bank your distraction to plant the knife
Blade of deception in brain of soot
The Mocking Jay, we pray, is the one you'll shoot...

When the sleeping giant wakes
Truth will stand in stalwart grace…

We count on your apathy o' little ones
No hope to change your pitiful fate
Pester not your dark lord's reign
Ignore the Mocking Jay's alarmed state...

For we're the fully sullied politico cast
We'll kill your future and lower your class
To liven our fortunes we now amass, and…

One day we'll murder that Mocking Jay ass!

***

- 17 -

The Redemicans

Again, the words must be said! The utter lack of understanding the average American has today of politics is amazing and dangerous. Ignorance is fertile soil for tyrants. The most stupid statement I ever heard was when a friend said to me, "Oh, we're not 'interested' in politics." When I asked her if she voted, she smugly replied, "Every election!" When I asked her how she knew she wasn't voting for bad things or bad people, she thought deeply for a moment, and I saw a dawning epiphany light up her face as she replied, "Oh... I just vote Democrat because my family always voted that way..." There are no words to describe the sublime stupidity in her grin of intellectual triumph...

To frame a second example... I once spoke with a girl who actually believed the two parties were like giant opposing armies on the field of battle... A titanic struggle between good and evil, and of course, she thought the Democrats represented good and the Republicans represented evil. She actually believed this! Oh boy...

When I explained to her that many Republicans and Democrats enter congress as middle class workers, and somehow exit 20 or 30 years later multi-millionaires, she simply couldn't believe it. She actually held in her heart that the Democrat Party was some kind of bastion of greatness dedicated to defending the poor, infirm, and minorities. When I proved to her they were mostly a bunch of race baiting hucksters who were getting rich just like much of the Republican elite, she broke down in tears...

Pressing on, I explained that the notions of "Republican" and "Democrat" were simply kabuki theater for the consumption of mindless idiots. I pointed out that the true divisions fell along religious and philosophical lines: Christian vs Marxist, Progressive vs Conservative, Libertarians vs Classic Liberals...

Later she confided in me that her eyes were opened on that day and now she is a Christian and stalwart Conservative.

I assert to all my fellow Americans that you must educate yourselves, and then, go out and preach the word to the unknowing. For one person at a time is how *we will excise the Left and unite America again*...

***

We pubes be fierce guardians of the republic!
Us dims be the champions of home and hearth
Who to believe? Who deceives?
Which way should I vote?

They're one hoard of losers - I think now I'll barf...
We pubes will lower your taxes to keep you at pace
We dims will raise your bills to keep you safe
Yet they're all millionaires a year after the race
And we keep paying, and paying, enormous rates...

The dims say they're for the poor
The pubes claim on poverty they're at war
So why are the collectors at my door?
Truth be told they're a bunch of whores...

The pubes claim they'll give us border control
The dims say, "Erase the border." to our
collective sob
Yet my kids are on crack and their intellect lacks
And a fellow from Juarez just got my job!
Truth be told … they're a bunch of corporate
hacks…

The dims want my kids to learn Spanish
To know how to place condoms on bananas
And they taught little Sally she actually loves Tess
Little Johnny's on Ritalin and wants a dress
God has no place in this sordid mess!...

The pubes swear to fend off jihadies
But when I texted my son about Pilates
The feds broke in the door looking for Ben Laudie!
Grandma was strip searched at O'Hare
One size fits all - spineless cows, I do declare!
It's just all so damn freaking weird...

The dims swore I'd get free health care
Then I lost my 40 hour job and benefits
Now I can't afford a Band-Aid at a first aid clinic
Can you see why I'm such a damn cynic?
They claim they're at war but I hear they are cool
From the same boardrooms and ivy league schools…

From CNN to lobbyists to congressional majority
All Kabuki for the consumption of fools
Perhaps it is time to shut down the sorority
A new batch of leaders to push out the ghouls
Super-men and wonder-women –
with budgets accordingly
To take back our future from the corporate mules…

The sword will be raised - the pummel comes down
the pubes and dims will go to ground
But the mighty blade will be raised again
Over the heads of our foes abroad and within
The sleeping giant now be awake!
Depart from our shores you evil waifs...

You see, this is the truth, I do believe
The pubes and dims a ploy to deceive
They are one and one seeking control
Fat, dumb and happy - electorate be sold
"Death to America" as Alinsky foretold
Widescreens and iPads – our minds to dissect
Truly magical brain numbing runes
The people sing mindless tunes…

Beware of complacency ladies and gents
Demand your freedom from gender free scents
Take up the call for inalienable rights
There's your rescue from progressive might
Our future of late is all that's at stake…

Loved ones please awake!

***

- 18 -

Where Has America's Anger Gone?

I was beside myself with anger over the travesty of our government trading five Taliban generals for the deserter and traitor, Bo Bergdahl.

The media appeared entirely complicit in whitewashing this man - who got seventeen good men and women killed trying to rescue him after he deserted his post and defected to the enemy. I believe Obama should have been impeached on this one incompetent folly: trading five Taliban generals for a traitor.

The final insult was when our president paraded out Bergdahl's parents onto the Rose Garden. Tolerance and compassion are one thing, but this was simply a pandering, disgusting show.

From my study of history, down through the ages, this behavior is the first symptom of nation cancer. A people must be united - not in weakness and division, but in strength and prosperity... And yes, anger... anger does play a role! Remember, you can be so open-minded that your brains will fall out...

***

Where has all the anger gone?
Long time passing…
Where's America's Outrage now?
Long time passing…

Hear terror's cry – belay the soldier's song
We love our traitors – freedom soon be gone
Taliban dad in Allah's glow
Bearded and wise
Follow your conscience Bo…

Where has all the anger gone?
Long time passing…
Where's America's Outrage now?
Long time passing…

Betray your brother's kid
America's next to go
Islam righteous and Christians low
You're the darling of the Left
in Obama's afterglow
Desert, betray, go Bo go!

Where has all the anger gone?
Long time passing…
Where's America's Outrage now?
Long time passing…

Soon we'll be running the entire show
Your momma in a burka on afghan throw
Take we down America's Godhead
Enslave the heathens like Allah said

Where has all the anger gone?
Long time passing...
Where's America's Outrage now?
Long time passing...

Come back home Bo and start a cell
Bomb Baha'i and burn Catholic pews
Break in half the Liberty Bell
Convert the libs and build ovens for the Jews

Where has all the anger gone?
Long time passing...
Where's America's Outrage now?
Long time passing...

Brought forth from Taliban lips
Your new name now a Quran tip
Heathens getting weak – lost their wit
Caliph Americana in a little bit

Where has all the anger gone?
Long time passing...
Where's America's Outrage now?
Long time passing...

Now's the time my darling Bo
Betray your country, oh don't you know
77 virgins – how restorative!
Strike them down with a clever pejorative
Americana traitors – enjoy the show

Where has all the anger gone?
Long time passing…
Where's America's Outrage now?
Long time passing…

GO BO… GO BO.. GO GO GO…

***

- 19-

The Road To Disaster

This is another indictment of those who have conspired to dumb down our youth in America today. For the past three or four generations, most young people leaving school are utterly devoid of critical knowledge. I can't hammer on this hard enough: it is the duty of every learned adult and parent to insure their children have a full education that is unrevised, and provided with all the tools they'll need to see right from wrong and discern darkness from light.

Most of our youth are unable to name the vice president or even identify the three branches of government. Liberal or conservative, their abject ignorance (and arrogant smugness) has been manufactured by an agenda in our public education system. This is utterly horrifying, and today I can say we made a huge mistake by giving the vote to 18 year olds. Their brains are not fully developed and at 18, they are thinking about fun, dating, and partying - but not what is truly good for the welfare of the nation.

Tally Ho America! As we race down the road to disaster...

***

Politics just ain't for me
Still I vote would you believe?
Not a clue how things are run
Being cool is how he won

Intellect deep as a paper sheet
Can't even name one senate seat
I know football and how to tweet
Free healthcare – oh ain't life sweet?

As to the last election call
For me, my girl picked them all
Another brick on a faceless wall
A helpless rock - by nine I stalled

Intellectual smarts - or girly tarts
Math and English; just brain farts
Cannabis 101 paved my way
For strato lounge and Frito Lays

I'm never bored - a reveling fool
Sex-ed tips - multi-partners too
When they beg me – "please don't vote"
I shuffle on down to cast and gloat

Oh Politics just ain't for me
A dumb jackass is all they need
Scratch here, check there o' mindless lad
And don't dare leave a hanging chad

So now you know – truth be told
Our nation's sorry state…
Helpless rocks who've all been sold
They just pull the levers as they've been told

Back to bondage like the days of old

***

- 20-

Acadons

Since the 1960's something has been changing in many American colleges and universities. Hard work, ability, critical thought, all seem to be quashed now. The way for a student to amble through these days is to pander to the instructor's social and political proclivities - which are typically arch feminist, far left wing Marxist, on to outright hatred of America. All you need to fail is to espouse any manner of Conservative or Christian thought. This is how they are obliterating exceptionalism and independent thought.

Most of us relate to playing the game with left wing ideologues, but it seems to be getting worse with each generation. Our poor kids are just trying to navigate their way through college without being ostracized, humiliated, and having to endure the trashing of the values their parents gave them. All this, at the hands of pig-eyed Marxist fanatics. I'm not alone in this assessment...

This is for the heartless Dons of Academia...

***

Oh petty toiling pooteroos
Send your scratch tried and true
Our wrath returned in flowery muse
We left your prose in rancid loo, Ha!

For we're the witty dour in Ivory towers
Snotty Olympian scholarly guild
Entreat the sullied unwashed masses
Trash their work then off to classes!

You we judge with fearsome power
Mocking jays with biting glower
Be humble bauble in sorrow's sleep
Perhaps we'll knight you a pauper's crown
Or remand your etch to rubbish heap

Oh so sorry little clown
Your whimsy muse evoked a frown
Prose a rigid formulary dreg
The judgment be we vote you down
Neither acclaim nor golden egg

For we're the witty dour in Ivory towers
Snotty Olympian scholarly guild
Entreat the sullied unwashed masses
Trash their work then off to classes!

Next time plea to local bee
Your Pikie kin will jump with glee
In their cups they judge your solemn place
Rhyming limericks by witty waifs

For... We... Are...
The witty dour in Ivory towers
Snotty Olympian scholarly guild
Entreat the sullied unwashed masses
Trash their work then off to classes!

"Let them eat cake"

***

- 21 -

Digital Stories

Digital Stories is a cautionary poem. I thought of it while watching a film of an experiment involving cocaine and mice. The poor little creatures were caged and supplied with a water beaker laced with cocaine. Sadly, they kept taking the tainted fluid until they keeled over and died.

The effect of computers on our society (and young people in general) is similar. Our youth have been on electronic crack for a couple of generations now and it is turning them into helpless idiots. All one has to do is look at what's happened to attention spans over the past 4 generations. Research now indicates that iPhones and computers are actually turning off sections of the brain. Cognitive ability is declining. Long term memory is declining. Overall intelligence is declining. Situational awareness is being severely impaired. Critical thought used to be intuitive, but now it's being overtaken by social media trending. They have all the knowledge of mankind at their fingertips; yet they are the most docile and easily led generation in history. The result is a hobbled generation that can't think without their phones, and their ability to focus is so impaired that many can barely carry on a conversation.

The first verses of this poem came to me when a girl crossing the street while texting walked right into the fender of my car...

***

iPhone iPad iPod... what hath we wrought?
Their signature steeped in arrogant sins
Intellectually void – young brains to rot
Self-esteem accented with slack jawed grins

I speak to them of truth and God
Deadpan eyes and brain befogged
See they only wine and song – intellectual spaghetti
Lost in the screen - brain filled confetti

True conversation – the dying arts
All the knowledge of man left untapped
Generation of fools and lusty tarts
Tragedy of commons our youth entrapped

Get thee hence o' digital lords
You made your billions on Classic Shell
New we unplug the enslaved hoards
Remand thy souls to Project C hell

The little screen we'll make a bore
Our children's hearts returned to the Lord
Back to camping, hiking, and family lore
Above all - God – America restored
As for you clever frog-eyed clicking bug

This digital story will fleece your nest
Take up your screen o' mindless slug
Darken no more America's best…

There is so much to be gained from proper use of the Internet. Don't waste your valuable youth on texting, twitter, and mindless dither on YouTube and Facebook.

Use the internet
to learn, to know,
to find the truth

***

- 22 -

Middle Management

Everyone, at one time or another, has fallen under the hegemony of an ignorant, self-absorbed, incompetent middle manager. You know, the sub-moron (with power) who does things like force an entire department to sing corporate jingo's in team building exercises... I've had my fair share of this garbage, and you probably have too. I dedicate this poem to the plight of victims not yet freed from the mindless middle manager...

***

You always strive to be the best
You're only here at the CEO's behest
So drive the ranks with zeal and zest
They'll never know your feathered nest

Why can't the toilers see my plan?
Split infinitives for the dullest man
Initiative ha! Don't they get paid?
Nose to the grindstone o' mindless sheep
My brilliance churns as the tea bag steeps...

Under my direction you thrive, I say
Away from the heat and light of day
The course I've set your only bet

Defiance crushed then doc your pay
Elbow grease truly sustain
Nether an extra farthing to toilers in need
Indifference to thrift, effort, and pain
Behold the truth in my dark disdain

Never empower - always ensnare!
I'm a Middle Manager, I do declare!
Drive in the wedge o' hapless peers…
My stately intellect so bright and fair

Come hither me drones - endure my tome!
For the secret I bare ye toilers seek
This place of woe your second home
Some served longer but they are weak
Pitiful old mares thein hope is bleak
I hold the power like lightening streaks…

Yer just a bunch of toiling sots
Cattle I drive around the lot
But I am brightened to the powers that be…
Of the sprightly, tightly, clever tree
Born to sing management songs…
The ruling class – oh can't you see?

For I'm the middle manager who's oh so cool
A ruthless backbiting grinning fool
Fear my power and stringent rules
It's my career and you be tools

Gather ye dogs – its training day
I lift thee up but ye be kept
Such passion in my brightened way
I heard thee not when you wept
Grace and hope at my behest

You're my static, feeble, sullen, tools
Now your God change all the rules…
Gripped with pain in heaving chest
My reign at end? Thy surly jest!
To bear the shame before you all
To pauper's grave I go to rest

Suffer me now a cooling drink…
Lazarus's lesson my fate be cast
No mercy for my life of stink
Stricken low – eternal last
Damned to hell in one-eye wink!

Remember that the middle manager is only a person. With hard work and your good efforts, you can rise above them!

***

- 23 -

The Crisis Manager

Millions of good people, Liberal and Conservative, have actually been tricked into thinking they're less than the *"clearly capable Crisis Manager,"* AKA the burrowed-in little rat who purposely mangles systems so only he or she is capable of fixing them when they break. Sometimes I wonder if they break on their own or get a little help now and then from the aforementioned... Meanwhile, good people struggle in the mess these job-security-trolls foist upon them. And when the system does break - regularly on cue, in rushes the hero.... Behold! The Crisis Manager is here with the big fix! In a sane world the Crisis Manager would be unnecessary, that is, if they knew their job in the first place... Relate?... I damn these parasites to the 8th Circle of Hell – right beside the child molesters and used car salesmen...

***

I've carved a niche for all to see
By complicating simplicity
No one can know what I hath made
Not to threaten my lofty perch
I hide the fix – so I they bade

The secrets I guard in my trashy office
Forbidden knowledge for my coffers
When things break – dare you not, novice
I'll leave this job for better offers

While the lower struggle
With things that should be no trouble
Sally forth I, the shinning knight
To save the day in majestic light

The lower befuddled and very, very troubled
On looking peers see but struggle
They know not my secrets – nor the knots I've tied
Competence befuddled – as the fix is applied

Know ye the price that must be paid
For I truly commit grievous sin
To block the rise of better men
But I must eat, so I will win…

A clever approach - cloying and pious
Chit chat jokes, band of brothers, sisters and others
Praise in the highest!
Truth be told, pink slip them all
If I had my druthers

Soon the day cometh when my better arrives
One who earnestly strives to set all things right
Untangle my befouled nest – I'll never survive
For the Crisis Manager withers; know-how derides

For on that day with stealth and fret
I take my secrets and strike at the threat
All ye see how evil this new man be
He can't do the job – the system's upset
He might even be a thief - don't you see?

He's mean and biased and prone to whim
To hell with his family - banish him!
Strike quickly and without regret
Excise the infection, the very best bet

Every good deed I try to do
There's this hulking lumbering fool
If this shall stand what becometh me?
The plant goes down for eternity

The end of my tome for those likened to I
Should chill to the bone with great surprise
For the righteous will stand against the evil man
And the pit that I dug I find myself in

The righteous rulers exposed my ploy
Condemn this good man? They fervently cried
My deceitful guise now before their eyes
Hostility exposed, and they know all my lies

And in the end, on unemployment and public shelter
I resolved to find God for forgiveness and cleansing
My soul's dross cleared in heaven's smelter
Made mends to my peers with nether a mincing

For in this brief life we are distracted with self
Sowing strife, dismissing the humble, wrecking life
All the while, blinded to eternity's fearsome embrace
I've returned to God - free of disgrace

Be humble, lift up your brethren in their struggle
Encourage the faithful – for selfishness leads to hell
Follow God's good path with thine own free will
Or prepare for the depths where your soul be stilled

Yet in the end, it is you my friend who must
choose

***

- 24 -

The Minimalists Are Coming

I'm sorry, but I like my comforts and pleasures. I love new products and abundance. I love invention, thrift, and hardworking savvy business people. Damn the minimalists and to hell with "The Story of Stuff !!"

Long live Cadillac's, locomotives, NASCAR, and Harley Davidsons!

How about we send the Minimalists to Antarctica? They'll be so at home there, won't they?

***

Tweet thee sweet and empty air
Facebook page of baying mares
Sleep on floor for we don't care
We'll give away your stolen wares

For we're the masters of minimization
Reject we plastics and mechanization
Dissolve we all the capitalist nations
A pox on earth - abomination!

Get thee hence from flashy car
Abate your stucco pitch and tar

Wooden spoon to slurp your muck
Meat and grain? - you're out of luck!
The Tech advance we'll surely destroy
For having nothing be pure joy
Plastic lives the Devil's ploy
Entreat you nothing girls and boys!

For we're the masters of minimization
Reject we plastics and mechanization
Dissolve all the capitalist nations
A pox on earth - abomination!

Hark! We're foiled by corporate plot
To push thin air be quite a lot!
We need iPhone and hotly spots
And Tesla motors to stop the rot

Entreat thee you our valid excuse
Offensive thee - we ply abuse
Take your wares to save the earth
A lovely smugly ironic ruse

For we're the masters of minimization
Reject we plastics and mechanization
Dissolve all the capitalist nations
A pox on earth - abomination!

Trust we children of Gia Earth
Hear we mighty master greens
We know what's best for you and yours
Buggy, horse, and wrapped in furs

For we're the wise and chosen few
Enviro snobs green and true
Stewards of earth which we'll renew
Your life or target tried and true

For we're the masters of minimization
Reject we plastics and mechanization
Dissolve all the capitalist nations
A pox on earth - abomination!

Simple Simon says: "what easy fools..."

***

- 25 -

First They Came For The Loggers

I patterned this after a famous poem by Friedrich Gustav Emil Martin Niemöller. However, his cautionary tale was about the German Nazis coming for the Jews and Communists. His message was powerful, but today the danger comes from Progressives Leftists.

Liberals and Conservatives have always been here and, believe it or not, we are a natural pairing. My mother was classic liberal and my father a Christian conservative. We need each other. Liberal and conservative pairing is the natural order of a free people. Our collaboration created the most powerful and prosperous nation since the dawn of civilization. However, western society has been infected with a cancer born of angry Leftists, and these apostates seek to destroy our union.

You can always differentiate a Leftist from a Classic Liberal because Classic Liberals are about freedom and unity. Leftists are about control and division. Their hallmarks are intolerance, anger, and the innate ability to magnify a social crisis; rubbing soars raw until people are rioting and at each other's throats. They are trying their utmost to divide us, ruin our great economy, and bring down the entire American construct.

I hate the Leftists – to a one… Sadly, they have penetrated the American Media, Academia, Hollywood, and the legal system, and today they effectively control the message in popular culture. However, they are still the minority, and it is up to us; people of good heart and strong conscience to undo their evil works the world over… starting with America and Europe…

***

First they came for the northwest loggers and I did not a thing though I'm a well-known blogger…

Then they came for Gibson Guitar and I thought, gosh be darn, I can't fiddle a yarn…

Then they came for Bodega Bay Oyster Farm and I pursed my lips – aren't those shuckers ocean raping suckers?…

Then they shut off the water to thousands of farms and I yawned a little – it can do no harm…

Then they came for the ranchers and I turned my head to mind my toddlers, banning beef be green men's fodder…

Then they came after the energy folks, and I ignored
the tale – for America has ethanol by the pail

Then they came for the power companies and I
fatefully remembered my environmental training -
and shut the lights till darkness waning...

Then I looked at my life and realized that all along
they had been coming for my family and me...but I
just couldn't see it...

Low supply and high demand, was always part of
their lively plan - to minimalize life and empower
them...

Every day, in every way life gets worse. Thousands
of hard-earned dollars gone to dirt. High prices, gas,
electricity, food... the more they take, all the good...
We chose corporate green, but handed them more
power to make our lives even more dour...

The government spies and controls nearly every
aspect of our lives. We can no longer afford a future.
Our kids have no work – my spirit is in sutures.
Trillions in debt and no way out. Soon to foreclose,
our enemies shout...

You fell in love with politicians, but didn't they
break your heart? Did you know they owned them
from the very start?...

We fooled your friends and unions bent.
The professors - useful idiots that we sent…

Even with all the knowledge of
Mankind at our fingertips, our minds were lost…
Poor little dimwit, too late now
Disaster cometh o' blinded cow…

***Every step pushing national loss! Your America?
We think not. We own you now…***

***

Epilogue

My final observations regarding the erosion of America's social norms is that there is a reason the Left has been so successful in penetrating nearly every institution, and practically obliterating our way of life and traditions. The key is very simple. They overlook their differences and stick together.

On the other hand, conservatives are a very weak amalgam. Perhaps because independence and self-sufficiency are in our DNA. Nevertheless, we are an easily divided construct. Consider the broad spectrum that makes up American conservatives... it ranges from hard core right-wing survivalists to the ballerinas in charge of the Republican party. I'm speaking of those daintily tip-toeing GOP senators and congressmen who can't seem to find the courage to take a stand on anything, including all the issues we elected them to address. The past couple of general elections have made it abundantly clear that we will no longer tolerate being backstabbed on immigration, border security, socialist health care, sovereignty, taxes, and big government, and so be it! If they don't come around, we will continue to stay home on election day. Tragically, that is precisely what gave us Bill Clinton and Barack Obama. And it appears they are dead set on helping Hilary win in 2016 too. That definitely explains the Trump phenomena, but our rallying point should be the ousting of our own party leaders. The sooner the better I say!

However, the problem goes far deeper than that. I have many liberal friends because they truly are more forgiving. Conversely, I routinely have trouble with my conservative friends due to various disagreements on the issues. For instance, I had a dear Catholic friend nearly write me off because I suggested the current Pope was a leftist, and that Catholic charities played a big role in illegal immigration. He was vehemently against illegal immigration but had a blind spot where the church was concerned. I lost another of my pals because I proved to him that marijuana is a dangerous drug. He smoked it on occasion, so I supposed I made him paranoid. Intolerance of our own is our Achilles heel!

Conservatives need to come together around a few core principles. We absolutely should take a stand on the social issues, i.e. God, abortion, and the evil of same-sex marriage. And it is a no brainer that preserving our institutions and removing government from our schools, is paramount. It should be a key plank of the party to obliterate the IRS, EPA and BLM. And securing our borders is critical. Along the lines of an actual immigration policy, we might come together around the notion of actually screening legal immigrants before they come here and return to taking only those with skills to offer. These are the big ones but there are many, many more.

My last words go to the huge effort so many have put into producing this book – primarily my beautiful and brilliant wife who was indispensable in producing and editing this work.

I beg you to spread the word. Send copies to people. Gift it on holidays. Buy it for friends and, by all means, leave it on the desk of people you can't stand...

God bless you loved ones. Together, we will win the fight one heart and one soul at a time. We can take America back. It isn't too late. We must come together, stick together, stay together, and in the end ...we will win.

TC

ABOUT THE AUTHOR

Who is Titus Corleone? Will we ever know who Titus Corleone is? The answer to that question is a resounding, yes, that is, if the reader truly wants to know the answer.

There is a spirit to America that is endowed by God, and that powerful force is awakened every time our beautiful nation faces danger. Titus wants you to know that today, we are in extreme danger and the Spirit of America has awakened with terrible resolve…

Titus Corleone is part of that resolve, and invites you to join him. He is a patriot who has served in the military; police departments, school districts, universities, and scientific research institutes. Today, he advises law enforcement, media agencies, and panels of medical providers. During the course of his career, he realized that America is under attack and is being dismembered from within.

The mission of Titus Corleone is to save our beautiful country by exposing the apostates undermining our history, and all our great traditions.

They are corrupting our institutions, churches, popular culture, and legal system. They seek to destroy our powerhouse economy and ruin the family system. This is a cage fight, and we're inside with the enemy - but Titus wants you to know that they are cowards and we are still the vast majority.

Titus invites you, begs you, and pleads with you to find a path to God, or if you've strayed away, return to Him. You are encouraged to join the fight to save America. God has blessed this nation with a great spirit. It is a gift from on high, and the Lord's message is this: "You will lose this house I have given you if you will not fight for it…" Add this book to your arsenal of intellectual weapons as you sally forth and lure the gullible back from the enemy.

DISCOVER

TITUS CORLEONE
www.tituscorleone.com

Also visit Titus on Facebook
or catch him on Twitter

www.ingramcontent.com/pod-product-compliance
Lightning Source LLC
Chambersburg PA
CBHW032030290526
45786CB00011B/1277